# FINGERPRINT
# & DRAW
## ·ON THE FARM·

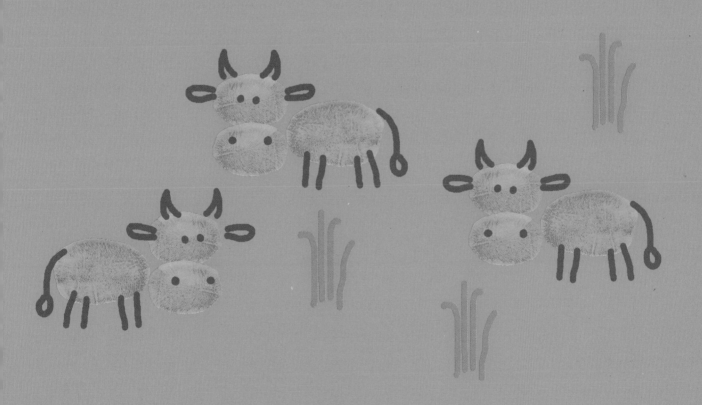

Walter Foster
Jr.

MAÏTÉ BALART

# TABLE OF CONTENTS

## HERE ARE ALL THE ANIMALS AND CHARACTERS YOU WILL FIND IN THIS BOOK!

Quarto is the authority on a wide range of topics.
Quarto educates, entertains, and enriches the lives of our readers—
enthusiasts and lovers of hands-on living.
www.quartoknows.com

© 2017 Quarto Publishing Group USA Inc.
Published by Walter Foster Jr.,
an imprint of The Quarto Group
All rights reserved. Walter Foster Jr. is a registered trademark.

Translated by Juliet Lecouffe.

The original French editions were published as *Les animaux de la campagne* and *Jeux de mains*.
© 2014, Mila Éditions – 2ter rue des Chantiers, 75005 Paris

Thank you to Étoile.

6 Orchard Road, Suite 100
Lake Forest, CA 92630
quartoknows.com
Visit our blogs at quartoknows.com

MIX
Paper from
responsible sources
FSC® C101537

Printed in China
1 3 5 7 9 10 8 6 4 2

# TOOLS & MATERIALS

ALL YOU NEED IS YOUR HAND, PAINT, AND A PAINTBRUSH TO GET STARTED.

FOLLOW THE SIMPLE STEPS TO CREATE EACH CHARACTER. USE MARKERS OR CRAYONS TO COMPLETE EACH PICTURE. THEN DRAW A FUN SCENE AROUND THEM.

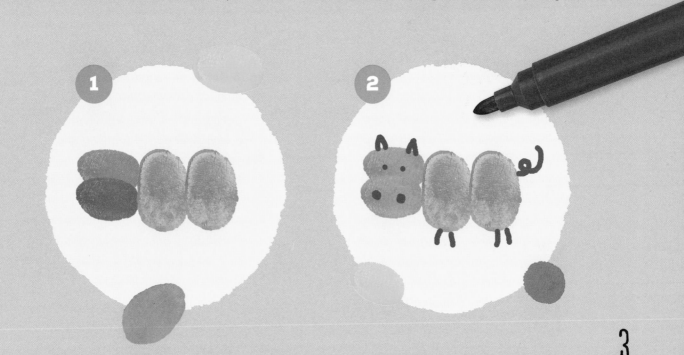

# ROOSTER & CHICKS

1

2

3

# COOPER THE ROOSTER TEACHES THE NEWBORN CHICKS HOW TO CHIRP.

# TURKEY & GOOSE

THE HIGH-SPIRITED
GEESE PARADE
IN FRONT OF GOBBLES
THE TURKEY.

# SCARECROW & CROWS

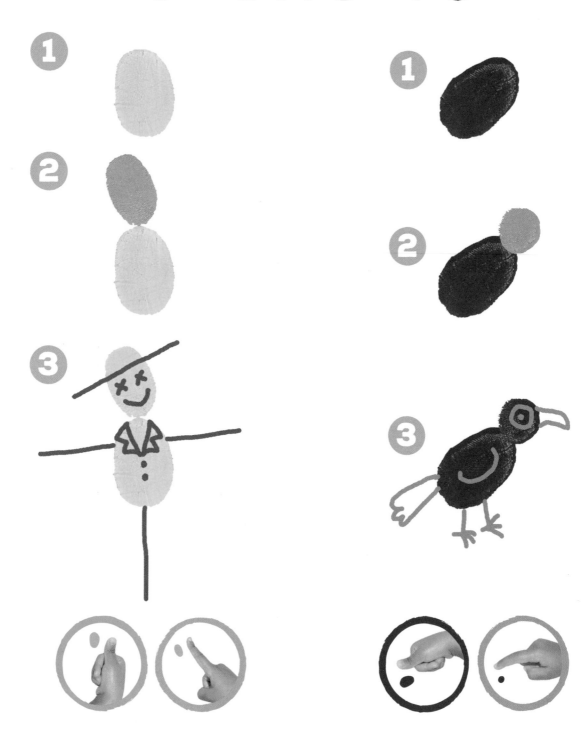

# STEVE THE SCARECROW DOESN'T FRIGHTEN OFF THE BIG CROWS.

# GOAT & COW

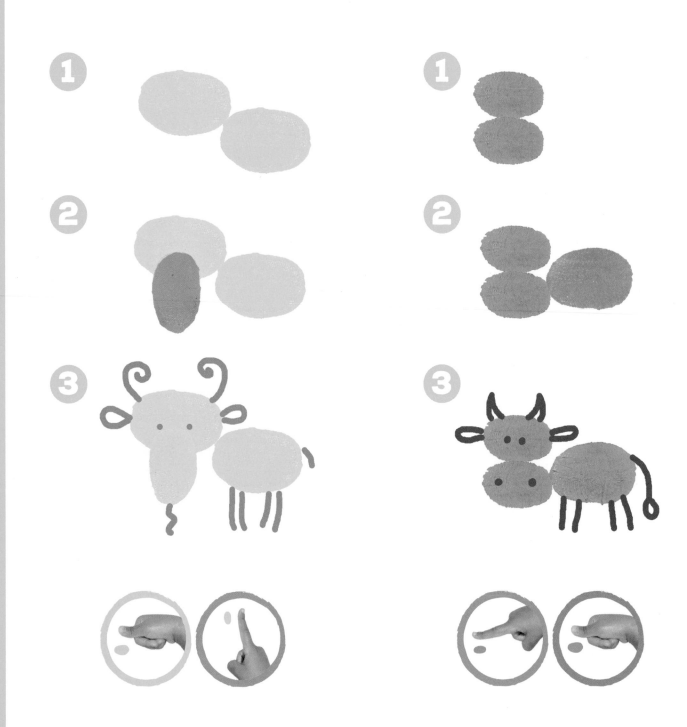

# DAISY, BUTTERCUP, AND GERTRUDE THE COWS INVITE THE GOATS INTO THEIR FIELD.

# BULL & CALF

BILLY THE BULL PLAYS WITH CHRIS, CASEY, AND COREY, HIS LITTLE CALVES.

# PIG & HEN

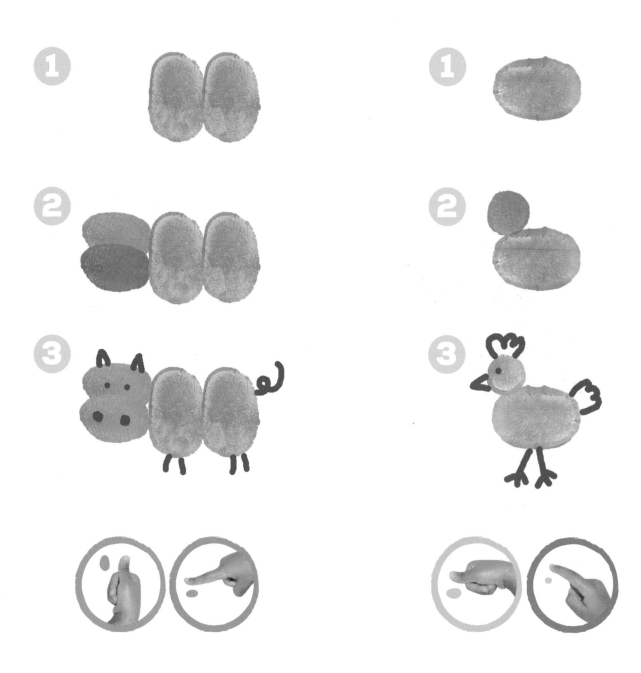

# STIG AND TWIG THE PIGS
## SNACK ON THE CHICKEN FEED.

# SOW & PIGLETS

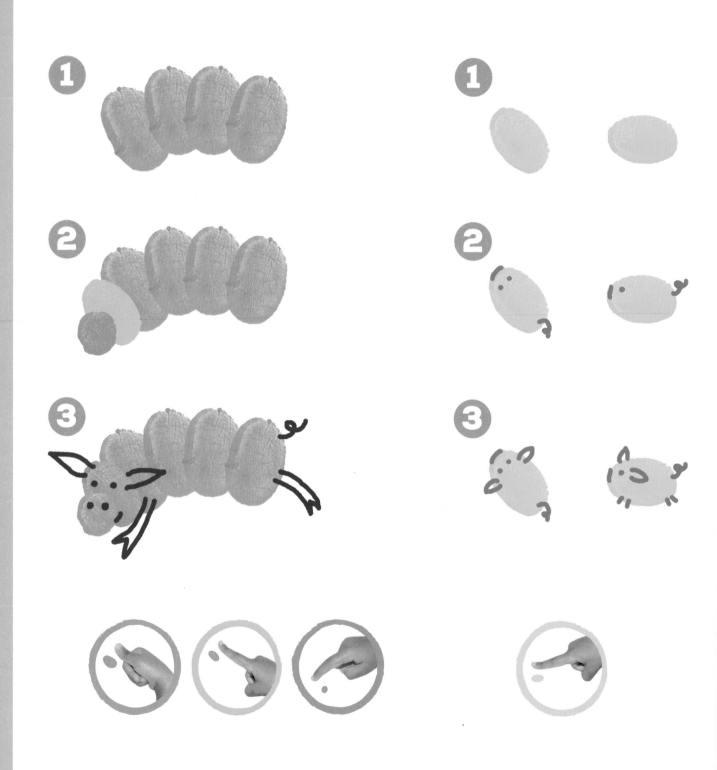

IN THE PIGSTY, SOPHIE
THE SOW FEEDS HER PIGLETS.

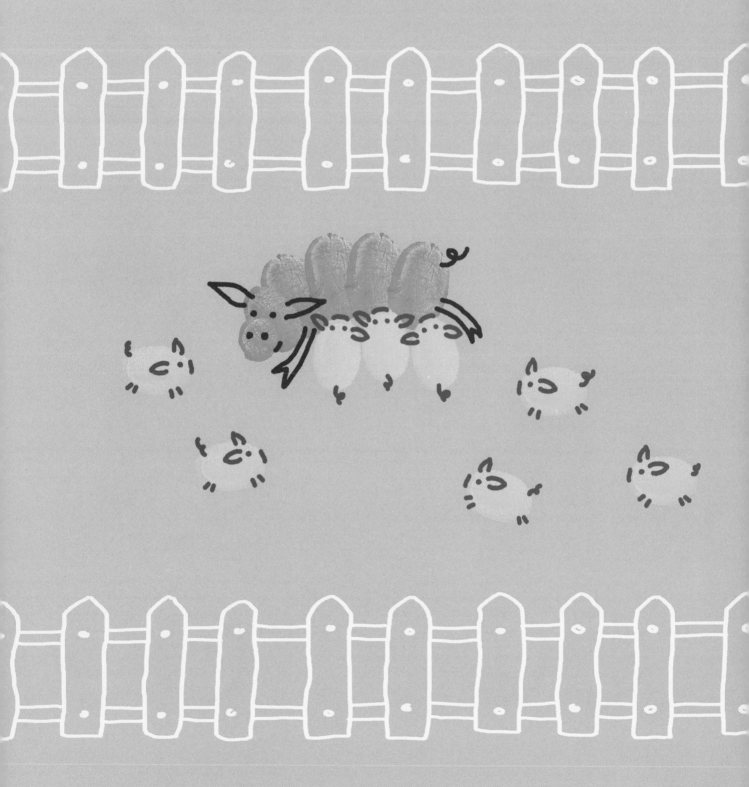

# TRACTOR & MILL

**1**

**2**

**3**

**1**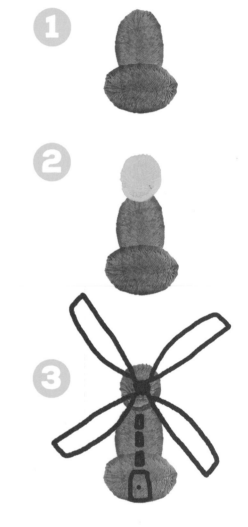

**2**

**3**

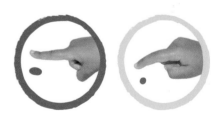

# THE TRACTOR GOES BACK TO THE WINDMILL TO DROP OFF THE GRAIN.

# FARMER & WIFE

# THE FARMER AND HIS WIFE
# ARE BUSY ALL DAY LONG.

# CAT & MOUSE

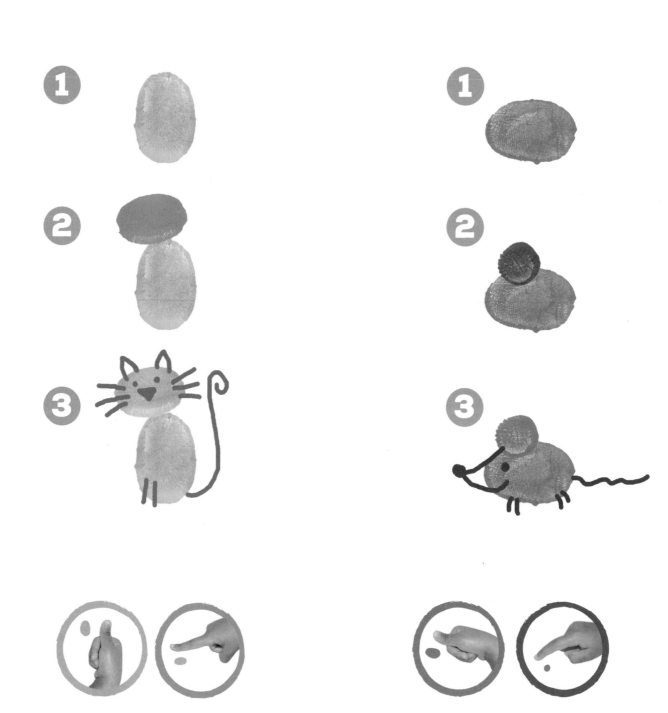

CHARLIE THE MOUSE
AND HIS FRIENDS
ARE NOT AFRAID OF
SCOUNDREL THE CAT.

# DOG & RAM

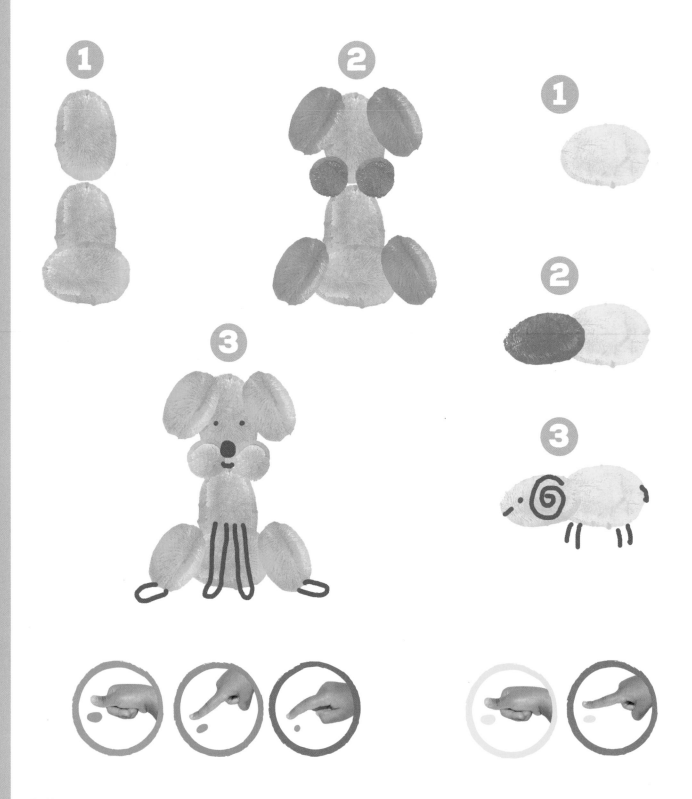

24

# SAMMY THE SHEEPDOG WATCHES OVER THE RAMS.

# FOX & RABBIT

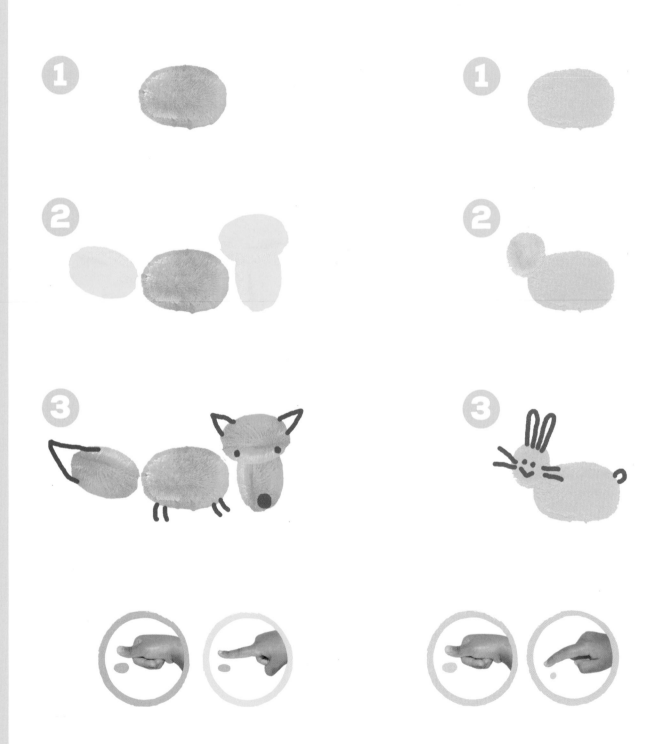

# FREDDIE THE FOX WANTS TO CATCH ROXY AND RUBY THE RABBITS.

# APPLE TREE

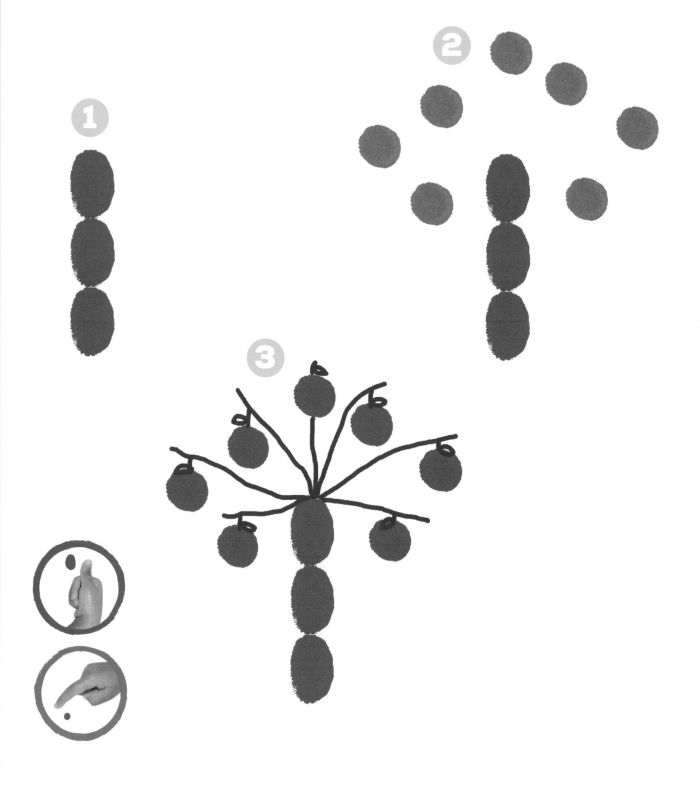

# IN THE ORCHARD, THERE ARE SOME LOVELY APPLE TREES AND LOTS OF APPLES TO PICK.

# CORN

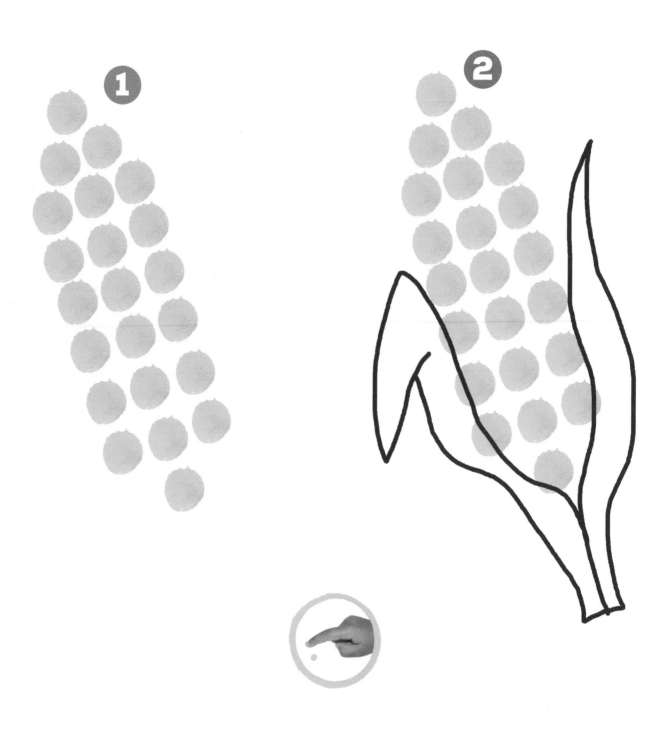

THE CORN IN THE FIELDS
LOOKS DELICIOUS.

# MOLE & FLOWER

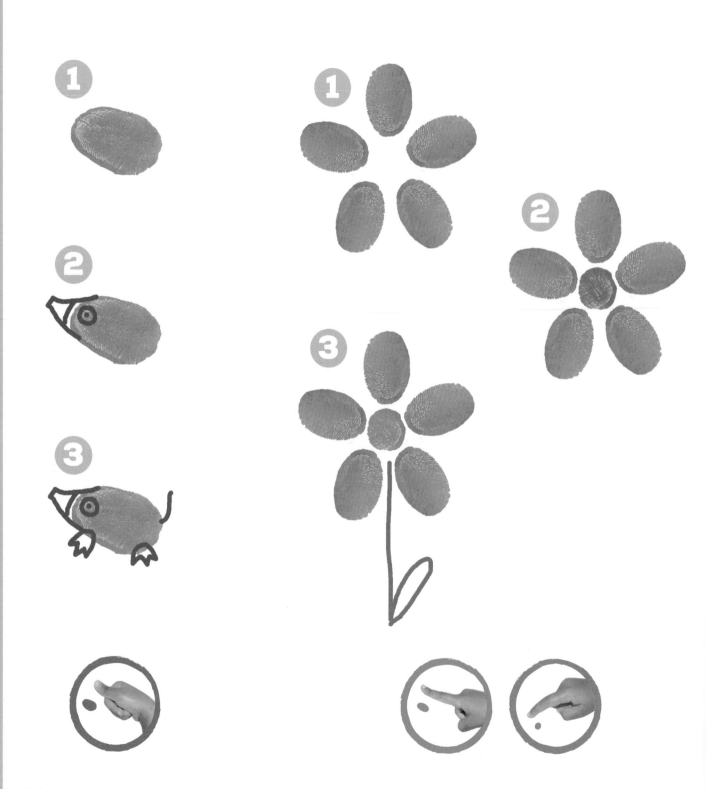

# MOLLY THE MOLE SMELLS EVERY FLOWER SHE PASSES.

# WOLF & SHEEP

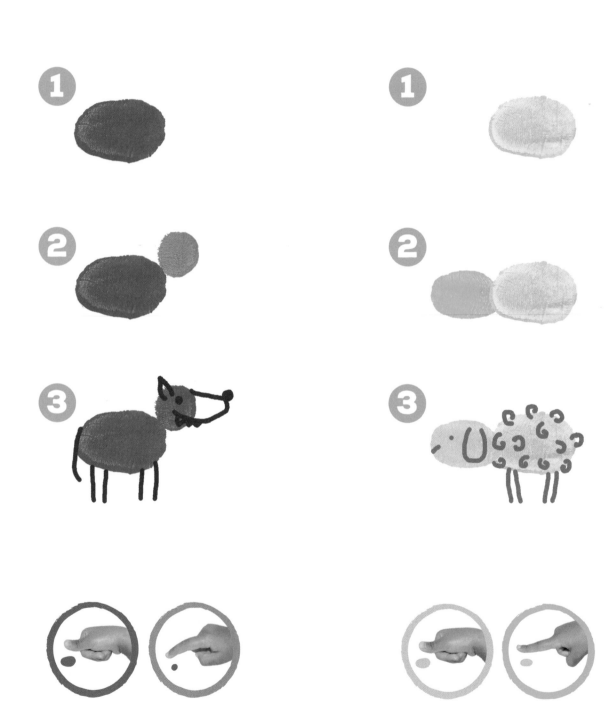

WATCH OUT, LITTLE SHEEP! WINSTON THE WOLF IS WATCHING!

# DONKEY & HORSE

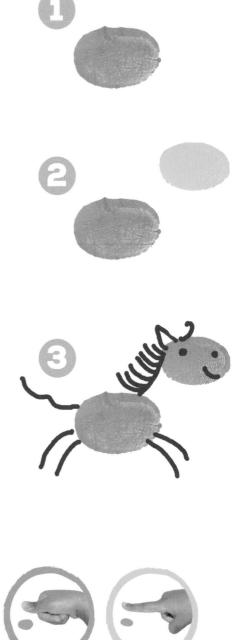

OWEN THE LITTLE DONKEY ADMIRES
THE HORSES AS THEY GALLOP PAST.

# SQUIRREL

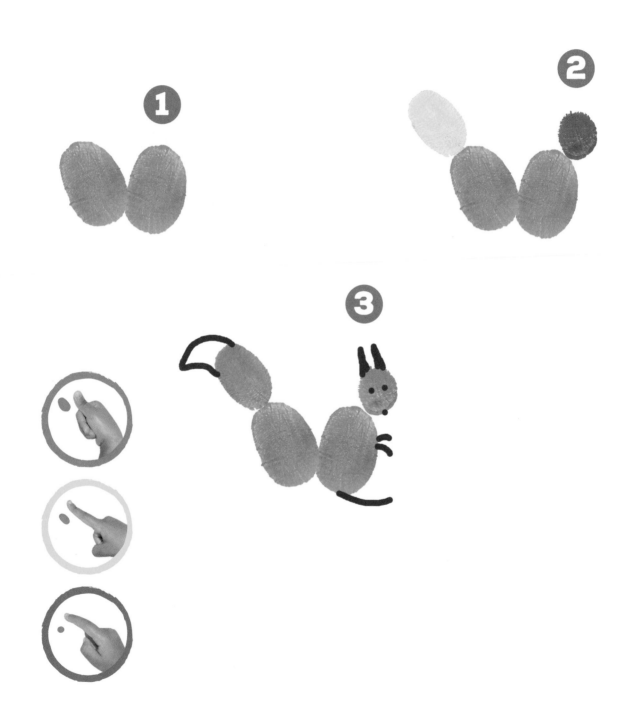

CYRIL AND LUCY THE SQUIRRELS
CHATTER ON THEIR TREE BRANCH.

# HEDGEHOG & OWL

**1**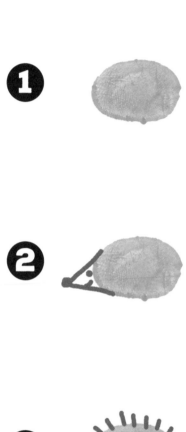

**2**

**3**

**1**

**2**

**3**

AT NIGHT, OLLIE
THE OWL KEEPS AN EYE ON
THE BUSY HEDGEHOGS.

# SWAN & DUCK

DONALD, DAVID,
AND DANIEL THE
DUCKS ADMIRE THE
GRACEFUL SWAN.

# TOAD & REEDS

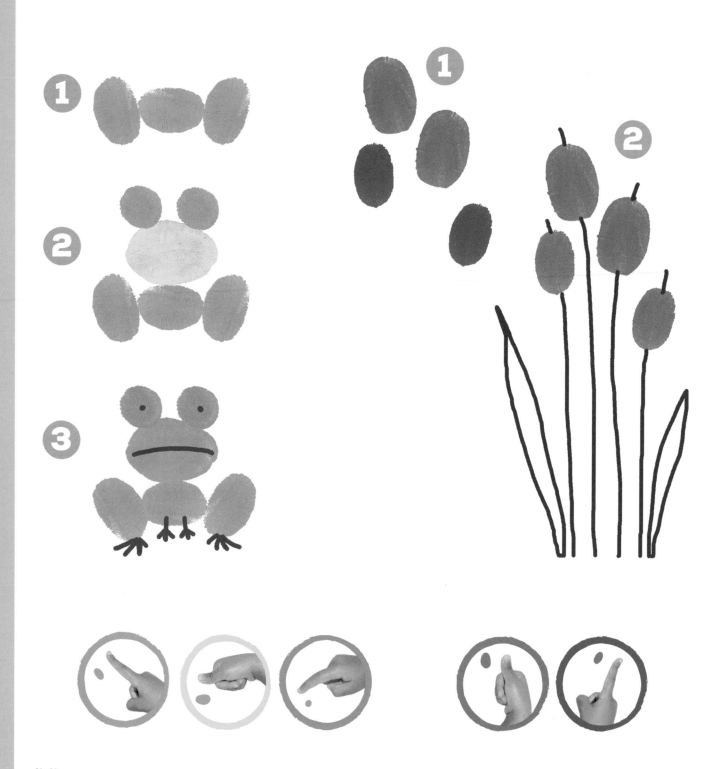

# TOM AND TIM THE TOADS
## HOP UNDERNEATH THE REEDS.

# LIZARD

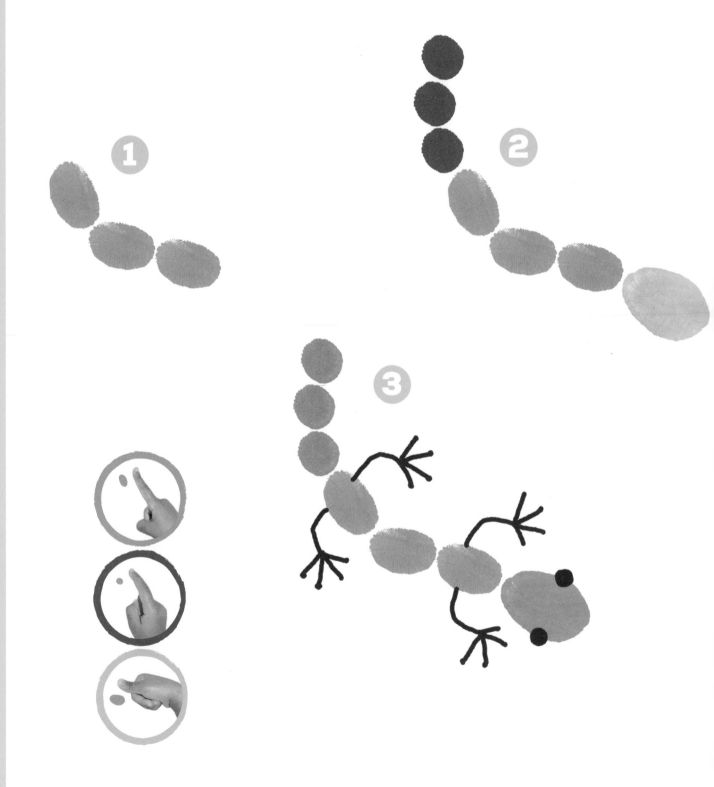

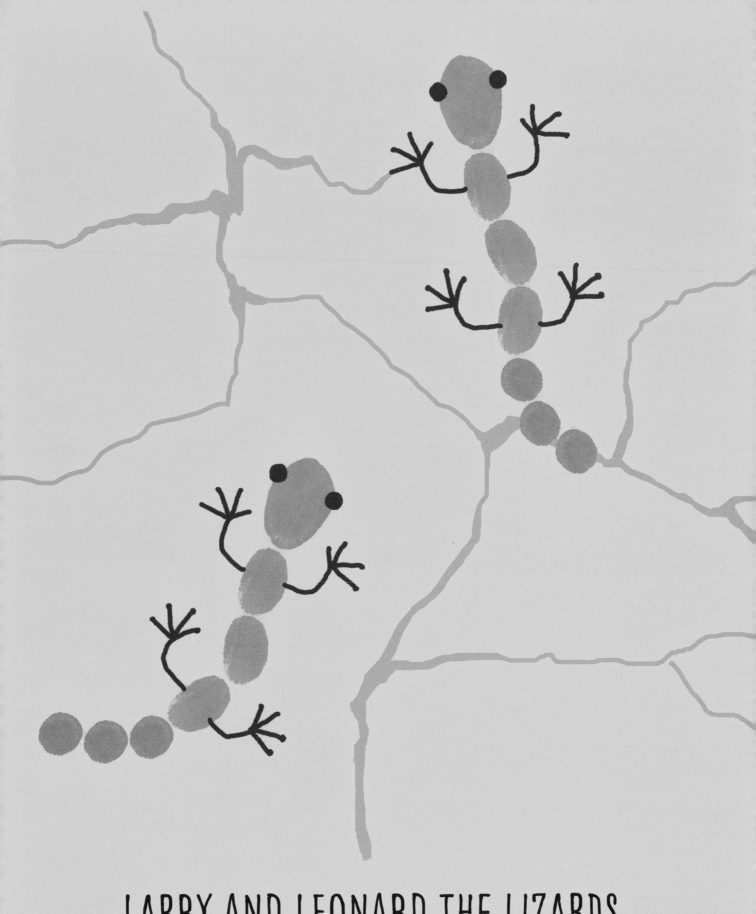

LARRY AND LEONARD THE LIZARDS
CLIMB UP THE CRACKS IN THE WALL.

WHAT OTHER CHARACTERS CAN YOU MAKE WITH YOUR FINGERS?

CREATE A FUN SCENE WITH ALL OF THE CHARACTERS
YOU HAVE NOW LEARNED TO DRAW!